Let's Plan A Banquet

Other books by
Dorothy C. Haskin

Tell Every Man: Conversion Stories
from Around the World

Successful Sunday School Teaching

Soul-Winning, the Christian's Business

Secret Meeting

Let's Plan A Banquet

by

Dorothy C. Haskin

Practical Suggestions for

    Banquets

    Potluck Dinners

    Hostess Suppers

    Afternoon Teas, Coffees

    and

Other Church-related Meal-meetings

Baker Book House • Grand Rapids, Michigan

Scripture passages from *The New English Bible,* © the
Delegates of the Oxford University Press, and the
Syndics of the Cambridge University Press 1961, 1970,
are used with permission of Oxford University Press.

Copyright © 1971 by
Baker Book House Company

ISBN: 0-8010-4025-6

Library of Congress Card Catalog Number: 70-176197

Printed in the United States of America

CONTENTS

And There I Was:

Everything has happened to me!

That is, at the church-related meal-meeting programs.

After having spoken at many meal-meetings, I remember the time when:

. . . the kitchen ran out of food and those who had been served had to wait forty-five minutes until food for the others was brought in from a nearby restaurant.

. . . the committee decided to serve only dessert instead of a meal and forgot to inform those who came with an appetite.

. . . whoever gave me directions to the church must have been confused, for after going miles out of my way I decided that each time the directions stated "right" I should have gone "left" and vice versa.

Having organized many luncheons, I remember when:

   . . . on two consecutive occasions the dish brought by the same person was either broken or ruined.

   . . . on two consecutive occasions the same person forgot to bring the dish she had promised.

   . . . on one occasion there was too much food and every night for two consecutive weeks I ate noodle casserole.

Everything can happen, and does, at the church-related meal-meeting program.

Therefore:

As experience teaches, "Wise men learn from the experiences of others, fools not even from their own."

Or as Scripture states, "The sensible man seeks advice from the wise, he drinks it in and increases his knowledge" (Prov. 16:21).*

This book is written with the leader (or chairwoman or president) and the committee members in mind, and I hope that all of you will avoid some of the pitfalls of the church-related meal-meeting program by profiting from the suggestions in this book.

---

*All Scripture is quoted from The New English Bible, unless otherwise stated.

1

Planning and Preparation

Yesterday, surrounded by encouraging friends, you agreed to take charge of the coming meal-meeting. (By this I mean a church-related meeting which includes both a speaker and refreshments, varying from the Dorcas Society luncheon to the yearly Mother-Daughter banquet.)

You accepted the appointment of president, chairwoman, hostess, or whatever title your group uses. It seemed such an honor! All your friends knew you could do it. Some because they didn't want the responsibility themselves and others because they truly did admire your sense of leadership.

But now it is morning — that cold grey

time which comes to all of us, when we marvel at our impulsiveness and wonder how we could have promised so much. Your husband has gone to work, your children to school; washing, ironing, cleaning, shopping, and that dental appointment clamor for your attention. You know you cannot do all the things which you hopefully promised. It is just too much. All right, face what is expected of you and see whether you can do it — for the Lord.

PRAY

The first step in undertaking any Christian responsibility is facing the Lord in prayer. Tell Him that you are afraid that you can't do it. He knows that, but it will help you to tell Him so. Then be willing to go ahead, for Scripture reminds us, "God is my helper" (Ps. 54:4). With renewed spirit and confidence in His help you are ready to begin.

START A PROGRAM NOTEBOOK

You will be more efficient if you make notes of the things which you have to remember to do.

List the following responsibilities, each on a separate page. Then as you continue you will have room to make additional notes under each heading. The headings should be:

Publicity

Decorations

Meal

Speaker

Music

Special Touches

All of these things, and many more, will be discussed, each in a suitable chapter.

PRAY

When you see all that has to be done you will again be sure you cannot properly do it all. But the Lord knew the details before you did, including the problems you don't know about yet. Remind Him of your inability. Soon you will realize that not only will He help but also your fellow committee members are standing by to serve. You don't have to do it all. This is a "fellow-workers" effort (See I Cor. 3:9).

APPOINT YOUR COMMITTEES

According to the size of your group or organization you will need:

Either one committee with a different member responsible for each task,

Or committees of two or three people responsible for each facet of the program.

Their responsibilities divide loosely into three parts: publicity, decorations, and kitchen. The duties of each will be discussed in a separate chapter.

You will be an ex officio member of each committee and expected to attend at least the first meeting and all other important meetings. When you go to the first meeting have a plan to suggest to the other members. You must be prepared to give them enough suggestions and enthusiasm to start them on their way. Otherwise, little may be accomplished.

LIST YOUR OWN RESPONSIBILITIES

Aside from being committee member ex officio or den mother to all committees, you are responsible for the following:

Speaker

Music

Special Touches

Your duties in each respect are discussed in a special chapter.

BE A PRE-HOSTESS

Extend as many personal invitations to the event as you can. People will appreciate being asked by the hostess and you will encourage the wavering ones to come.

BE A JACKER-UPPER

In a friendly way keep track of the progress of your committees and committee members. Phone them. Don't presume that you will meet those you want to see at church and that you can remind them then. They may not go to church that day. Or they may be across the room from you and, because you are delayed by someone else, they will be gone before you can reach them. Leaving anything to chance is risky.

However, checking up is a perilous occupation, requiring tact; so see the chapter on The Leader's Be-attitudes.

PRAY

By this time so much has been accomplished that you will begin to think that everything will go smoothly. This is the time to really pray for, as Scripture reminds, ". . . apart from me you can do nothing" (John 15:5).

2

The Leader's Be-attitudes

"I don't want to work with her. She's too bossy."

"I like to help her. She gets things done."

Which will the women say about your leadership?

That depends upon your ability to see yourself as the Lord sees you and under His guidance to improve your disposition and leadership qualities.

Most church women are more than willing to help with church-related activities but they perform efficiently only when they have a leader who is spiritually alert to the demands of leadership.

Being a leader requires you to ". . . be wary as serpents, and innocent as doves" (Matt. 10:16). You have an idea of what you want to accomplish, whatever it is, building up the local church or strengthening the missionary society, but you have to work with voluntary assistants, many of whom do not have your vision. If you don't lead with oil can in hand, they can quit and complain about you to everyone in the church or organization.

Leadership calls for disposition discipline. Therefore, your most important preparation is the development of your spirit. Here are a few proven attitudes which you must be willing to cultivate.

Blessed are the prayerful for they shall possess a quiet spirit.

Every religion recognizes the need of meditation, of being quiet before God. Surely, if prayer in some form is universally recognized as mandatory, it must be. The Christian religion especially stresses the need for a time of daily prayer. Prayer is the proper preparation for all Christian activity.

Willingness of spirit and ability to do, do not take the place of prayer. Pre-prayer will enable you to perform your tasks with serenity of spirit. Therefore, make prayer a daily diving board into your duties.

The Lord, centuries ago, told the prophet Isaiah, ". . . in stillness and in staying quiet, there lies your strength" (Isa. 30:15). The

Lord Jesus told His disciples, ". . . apart from me you can do nothing" (John 15:5). The same principle is true for the leader today.

Blessed are the prompt
for they shall accomplish much.

When you are elected president or appointed chairman of a committee, at that moment look around and see whom you can ask to help you. Don't delay. That night, before you go to sleep, make a list of the things you must do. Get going. The next morning, start doing your phoning, your shopping, or what have you.

If you ask a successful man how he managed to accomplish so much he will tell you, "When I had to do something, I did it promptly." Or "Whatever task lies to your hand, do it with all your might" (Eccl. 9:10).

We tire, not by the work which we have done, but by the work which nags to be done. Work is easy when you are ahead of it, instead of behind, chasing after it. It is better to be quick and make a mistake than to dally and accomplish nothing.

Make "Do It Now" the rule of your life.

Blessed are the brief
for they shall be listened to.

Usually the first of the four Gospels to be

translated into a foreign language is Mark, because it is the briefest of the four. Its brevity makes it effective.

But you protest "I want to be friendly." All right, be friendly but remember much that passes for friendliness is only muddled thinking. Train yourself to be brief. That will take clear thinking. Before you go to the phone to give instructions, or make an announcement, write down the salient points. If you do that, you will say all that is necessary without wasting your time and the time of your committee members.

As long ago as one hundred years before the time of Christ the Roman statesman, Cicero, said, "Brevity is the best recommendation of speech, whether in a senator or an orator." This truth is more widely known than practiced. Even about prayer, Doctor Martin Luther, the Great Reformer, said, "The fewer the words, the better the prayer." And the Bible says that we are not heard for our much speaking (See Matt. 6:7).

Blessed are the cooperative for they shall have help.

Don't try to do everything yourself. It will only over-tax you and weaken the confidence of your helpers. You may get things done the way you want if you do them yourself, but there is too much to be accomplished for one person to do it all. Besides, others need the opportunity to achieve. After all, executive ability is the ability to direct others to do the work.

Ask different people to take charge of the publicity, decorate the tables, make the place-cards, give the announcements, read the Scripture, perform the musical numbers, or what have you. After you have portioned out all the work you can, you will still have plenty to do.

Also, take every suggestion you possibly can. To do so encourages others and, who knows, maybe your helpers know something you don't.

> Blessed are the discreet
> for they shall have no enemies.

After you have asked someone to perform a task, let her do it in her own way. This is easier for both of you. Each person has her own individual style of working and can do things better in her practiced way. You should not be supervising her constantly, try-ing to change her work patterns. Her way may be even better than yours. Give her a chance. Watch and see how she does.

If, on the other hand, a person makes too

many mistakes, or forgets too often, say nothing, but don't ask her to help again. It is better to weed out the incompetent with silence than with scolding.

Blessed are the courteous
for they shall have many friends.

Watch the way you word corrections. Use the "Yes, but" technique instead of saying, "Don't do that" or "You're wrong." For instance, it is better to say, "Don't you think it would be easier, or quicker, if you did it this way?" Or you might say, "That is fine, but I would like to suggest __."

"Thank you" is a valuable word. When I travel to different countries, I cannot learn to speak the different languages, but I learn, in each, to say "thank you." I find that the use of it pleases people and consequently I make many friends.

Never speak crossly to those who help you, not even when several people are asking questions at the same time. You may have to bite your lips and wait before you answer, but in the long run, you will be thankful that you did.

As Scripture reminds you, "Let your conversation be always gracious, and never insipid; study how best to talk with each person you meet" (Col. 4:6).

Courtesy takes practice and restraint but with it you will win excellent workers.

Be ever mindful of the fact that you are working with volunteers who can quit. But you object, "I, too, am a volunteer. Don't I deserve consideration?"

Yes, you deserve consideration from the Lord, for by the time you are a leader you know that it is to Him, and Him alone, that you volunteered.

3

Food Ways to Friends

Sometimes I think we human beings do nothing but eat. We are constantly inviting friends to our home for "dinner." If someone stops for only a short time we offer him, "Coffee and __." Business is transacted over lunch. A man devotes his life to earning money first for food, and then for other things. One of a woman's chief responsibilities in life is preparing food.

The Lord Jesus was called many things, but among His titles is The Bread of Life (John 6:35). As Christians we celebrate His death and resurrection with Holy Communion which is, in a sense, a meal of bread and wine.

And why not?

Food is important.

Including water, it is the most important thing in the world. You cannot live without food and water. The type and quantity of food you eat contributes to the state of your health and your ability to enjoy life.

Therefore, if you hope to win friends to the visible church or any branch of it, your social planning must include food of some sort. The following are food ways to friends.

REFRESHMENTS

Often, mere refreshments are adequate, e.g., coffee hour after the Sunday morning service, youth meeting Sunday evening, a morning work meeting for women, an afternoon tea or an evening Bible study group.

The most simple refreshments require:

Coffee

Tea

Sugar

Cream or one of the dry creamers

Hot water for people who want their coffee or tea weaker than others

Milk, if children are present

Punch on hot days or for large crowds. (There are always some people who drink neither tea nor coffee.)

A sweet. This can be either a nut bread,

buttered or plain, a sheet cake, cookies, or a special cake or pie.

Here is a basic recipe for punch which is inexpensive and delicious, and which can be multiplied as many times as is necessary. The basic recipe makes three quarts or enough for six to eight people. Allow one pint to a person.

Pour 2 cups of tea on 2 cups of sugar
Add 1-1/2 cups orange juice
    1/2 cup lemon juice
    1 quart water
    1 quart ginger ale (shortly before serving)

For a special touch in a large punch bowl you can float scoops of sherbet.

For different ice cubes, pour water into trays or small cartons, add food coloring and a maraschino cherry or pineapple spear and freeze. These make the punch gala.

Be careful to keep the refreshments simple. Otherwise if each hostess tries to outdo the other, serving refreshments can become a vicious circle.

When planning refreshments it would be helpful if each woman in the group would take her turn, but ability, finances and dispositions differ. Therefore, let each woman volunteer for what she feels she is best able to do.

THE SACK LUNCH

This is the least interesting of all community eating. However, when there is work to be done, when people are on a hike, when some are on special diets, or when there is serious doubt as to the number of people who will come, it is the best solution.

Each person brings her own lunch in a sack. A hostess is appointed to furnish coffee or a soft drink and paper cups. Time for preparation and eating is thereby cut to a minimum.

One variation is to exchange sack lunches. It does add surprise and spice, but it should be announced ahead of time as a person will want to do a little extra when she knows her lunch will be exchanged.

THE RESTAURANT MEAL

In this day of the affluent society with more women having less inclination to do extensive cooking, church groups often have to arrange to have their breakfast, luncheon or banquet at a restaurant.

This is an excellent idea for men's breakfasts, for groups who want to eat together after a church service, or for any special occasions or Christian organizations who do not have local church members on which to call for help.

Naturally the selected restaurant must be first class and conveniently located with ample parking space. Phone several who specialize in groups for a choice of menu and price.

This way of eating is more costly than do-it-yourself meals because the restaurant must make a profit, and to their charge you must add a sum to cover additional expenses. The restaurant meal simplifies all service problems, but the draw-back is that it eliminates the fellowship of serving together.

However, if your group decides to go this way, skip the rest of this chapter and concentrate on the other chapters. You still have enough to do if you are to promote a satisfactory meal-meeting.

THE PLANNED MENU

This is the type of meal that is usually served when one hundred or more guests are expected. One menu is decided upon and the day is spent preparing it. It takes practice and the church who has this type of dinner frequently pays a hostess who supervises the entire dinner. Personally, I deplore the wilted salad and dry pie that greets one upon arrival but there seems to be no other way to serve a large group.

For your large group menu you will find a number of cookbooks in the public library or for sale at book stores with ideas for serving groups from fifty to one hundred. Use only tested and approved recipes to avoid unhappy failures.

Here is a suggested menu for fifty people.

Pot roast	20 pounds
Mashed potatoes	15 pounds
Carrots	18 pounds
	(allow 3 pounds for carrot sticks on relish tray)
Peas (frozen)	7½ pounds
Celery	4 stalks
Radishes	6 bunches
Lettuce	10 heads
Fruit cup	
apples	3 pounds
oranges	12
grapes	2 pounds
grapefruit	4 pounds
pineapple	1 large can
Ice cream	2 gallons or 7 bricks
Rolls	6 dozen

Besides you will need 2 pounds butter, 3 quarts milk for the potatoes, 1 quart coffee cream, flour, salt, pepper, 2 quarts French dressing, 2 pounds coffee, 15-20 individual bags of tea, 4 pounds of sugar.

Follow this
PREPARATION SCHEDULE
Table Service for Fifty at 7:00 P.M.

2:30 P.M. Brown meat on all sides, and put on to cook slowly

Prepare fruits for fruit cup and refrigerate

Prepare carrots, celery and radish roses and put in ice water

Prepare lettuce for salads and refrigerate

Peel potatoes, and place in cold water

4:30 P.M. Put water on to boil for potatoes

5:30 P.M. Start cooking potatoes

Peel and slice carrots

Allow ice cream to soften slightly

6:00 P.M. Put water on to boil for carrots, peas, and coffee

Cut butter into pats, arrange on plates, and refrigerate

Arrange relish dishes

Portion salads

Fill salad dressing cups

Fill fruit cocktail cups

Scoop out balls of brick ice cream and place in paper cupcake cups, return to freezer or coldest part of refrigerator until ready to serve

29

6:30 P.M. Cook carrots
         Cook peas
         Make gravy
         Prepare coffee
         Slice meat, and arrange in pans
            in portions
         Mash potatoes
         Drain and butter vegetables
7:00 P.M. Start serving meal

The actual serving of the main course is another problem. Often young people can be hired for a token wage. Or plans are devised where all the people facing the speaker line up to get the main dish from a serving table, while all the people with their backs to the speaker's table clear off the dishes and get the dessert.

The best variation of this type of dinner is to serve it smorgasbord or cafeteria style. The menu may offer a few simple choices, such as two salads, two meats, but not too many, for it is the hesitant choosing that slows up a line. But at least this way the salads aren't as wilted, the meat not as cold and the cake not as dry.

I highly recommend the use of paper service. Colorful napkins can be bought inexpensively. Do not buy cheap paper plates. They bend when the food is put on them. And be careful, buy the right kind of cups, special for hot or cold drinks. Plastic eating utensils are also recommended, especially if you buy the more expensive ones that you can wash and reuse. Paper service solves the clean-up problem almost automatically. You can toss the paper items in the trash and wash only a few kitchen utensils.

POTLUCK

The fellowship favorite.

All together now, we plan, we work and we enjoy ourselves.

The Unplanned Meal. The fun of potluck is that even though you don't plan it, but let each woman bring whatever she wants, it still seems to balance. All but the meat. Meat is expensive. People are slow to bring it. It is best to definitely plan the meat — even to paying for it.

Or you can make a list, and have different persons promise what they will bring, casserole, salad or dessert, and then watch the menu balance. As for the rolls, butter (or spread), and coffee, often one of the men or women who work all day will bring these non-preparation items.

Always expect a few people to come who bring nothing. Sometimes a friend wanders in, or someone who is doing something else on the program will decide that is sufficient contribution. Or you invite the minister or a bachelor or two. There is always enough.

The Salad Bar. This is a summer variation of potluck. Everyone is invited to bring her favorite salad and there is such a large variety of salads that a balanced meal results.

The Dessert Bar. This is another summer success. Everyone brings a different dessert: cookies, cake, pie, gelatin, pudding, or what have you. For an extra special dessert, see if you can have homemade ice cream. Surely a couple of people have ice cream freezers. But here, where two or three people are bringing enough for fifty or more people, the society should be prepared to pay for the ingredients.

Encourage those who bring the pastries to make extra so that after everyone is served you can sell the baked goods and make extra money. This is a day when fewer people are baking so many are pleased to be able to get something home-made to take home.

The All Together Meal. This is a planned variety of potluck. A certain menu is agreed upon, such as any one of the following combinations:

Spaghetti and orange gelatin salad
Tuna casserole and lime gelatin with pineapple and cottage cheese
Chili con carne and tossed salad

Stew and hot rolls

Macaroni with cheese and tossed salad

Different people agree to make one item each on the planned menu. One person is usually responsible to bring enough for eight people. Then you own or borrow an electric cooker and when the main dishes are brought, dump all of one kind together and heat. Though each person has made his share a little differently, they all blend together.

The Hamburger Meal. This is another favorite, if you can get two or three expert hamburger cooks. It takes practice to get enough of the hamburger ready at the same time.

Each person takes his own plate and roll from a table, then goes to the barbeque where the patty is put on the roll. Then he goes to another table where he builds his sandwich with mustard, catsup, lettuce, pickles, sliced tomatoes, sliced onions, or what have you. Potato chips should also be available.

Of course, beverages are available at all of these meals.

General Suggestions

When serving potluck, set up the serving tables so there can be two lines, one on each side, and someone directing people to both sides. Start with the plates and eating utensils. Then the salads and main dishes. Beverage is last so it won't spill. The dessert can be served later on a separate table.

Don't put all the food on the serving table at once. This only causes delay as people take too much time making up their minds. Those behind them in line are eager to make their choice also.

If there are salads, put one gelatin, one tossed, and one potato (or macaroni) out at a time. Appoint someone to watch and when a dish is nearly empty, put out another. If there are two tossed salads, when one is nearly gone, combine it with the new one.

The same is true of your casseroles, though you will probably need two at a time. Some people do not care for fish. Therefore if you have tuna casseroles and meat casseroles, put out one of each.

Warn your cooks to be careful of the seasoning. Never make anything highly seasoned. If onions are put in the salad, put up a small sign indicating that onions are included.

THE FOREIGN MEAL

These are interesting and should be tried occasionally, perhaps once each year.

Food is something that a person must learn

to like. A baby enjoys only milk. Then he is taught to eat bland food. Only gradually does he acquire a taste for spicy food as many foreign foods are. Therefore if you have a Mexican meal, or Italian spaghetti, or Indian curry, use less seasoning than the national preparing the same food would use. This meal will be easier to serve if you know someone from the country of the origin of the meal who will supervise. Otherwise, there are cook books containing foreign recipes.

An occasional foreign menu does add a piquant flavor to your church-oriented social season. See chapter on Special Occasion Banquets for ideas along this line.

FOOD FOR CHILDREN

This should always be the most simple possible menu. The best is:

> Hamburgers or hot dogs
> French fries or potato chips
> Catsup which they can apply themselves
> Pickles may be offered but olives are
> seldom eaten by children
> Milk or fruit punch

Cookies and ice cream, enough to cover Mount Everest. Dish it out ahead of time. Put a dipper full in each paper cup and put in the coldest part of the refrigerator. Then, at the last minute all you have to do is take them out.

"It is not the quantity of the meat, but the cheerfulness of the guests, which makes the feast" said Edward Hyde, First Earl of Clarendon, English statesman and historian (1609-1674), and it is still true.

4

Speaker — Handle with Care

Church-related meal-meetings are speaker-oriented. He is the big attraction, next, of course, to the food. Nothing is more important than food! But you can get food elsewhere. Therefore, the speaker often is the ingredient that changes the prospective attendant's answer from "Maybe I can come" to "Yes, I'll be there."

CONSIDER MANY POSSIBILITIES

Two seconds after you have accepted the chairwomanship of the gala event, start thinking about whom you will ask to be the main attraction.

Go to your pastor for suggestions.

Ask the past chairwoman and the heads of other organizations for suggestions.

Ask your friends, especially those who attend other churches and may know of different speakers.

Listen and consider all suggestions. Learn all you can about each person. Remember that a speaker belongs to a varied breed. He may come late, squirm during your announcements, advertise his own interests, and slip out before the closing prayer. Or he may arrive on time, be charming, be interested in everything that goes on, speak interestingly and stay afterwards to chat with his listeners. Invite the best speaker you can, accept his shortcomings and be thankful for his redeeming qualities.

BOOK IN ADVANCE

You will want to invite the speaker who is best known to your group because he will attract the largest audience. If you cannot get a speaker who is well known, consider his subject; is it popular? Right now drugs command attention. The subject must be of interest to your group. People are interested in themselves first of all and therefore topics dealing with family or personal problems are always popular.

In any case, the speaker will be in demand

by other churches and societies. Therefore, as soon as you have prayed sufficiently to decide who to ask, contact him so he can clear the date.

Tell him clearly what day and time you expect him. Once I came for a meeting at 9:30 in the morning, only to learn that I was expected at 9:30 in the evening. I had thought 9:30 was too late for an evening meeting but I had been invited to speak after the dinner and business meeting.

Explain what type of food will be served. Once I was invited to speak at a banquet and arrived hungry, only to be told that the committee had changed its plans and only coffee and cake were being served. Another time no preparation had been made for my dinner and as I spoke I grew so weak it was difficult for me to continue.

Agree on the amount of time to be allowed him. This is necessary because, while he may be a speaker who presents the same message every place he goes, he probably tailors it a bit for each gathering.

Ask for a "fact sheet." If the speaker is used to being invited to different gatherings he will have a fact sheet (or press release) telling the correct way to spell his name, his credentials and the title of his talk. This you will turn over to your publicity committee. (See chapter "Say It Right, Say It Often.")

MAIL DIRECTIONS

Do not try to give the speaker directions over the phone. They are too confusing. Mail them to him and, if possible, include a map.

Be clear as to the name of the town, the freeway off-ramp and the street location of the building where the meeting is to be held. Consider the possibility of another street with the same name in a neighboring town.

As a speaker I have often grown hopeful when I saw a freeway off-ramp with the name I was looking for, though it was not in the proper town (I didn't realize that). I turned off the freeway only to become so confused that I had to ask a service station attendant for directions, learning that I was miles away from my destination.

The Los Angeles area is a cluster of small towns with similar names, such as Montrose and Monrovia, including a number of freeway off-ramps with the same name. Your town may be located in a similar network, all bewildering to the stranger.

ALLOW THE SPEAKER SUFFICIENT TIME

I have driven a total of four hours, two

hours each way, and been allowed nineteen minutes to speak. The speaker has a definite point to make, and unless he makes it, his speech is valueless. Therefore, the average speaker should be allowed thirty or forty minutes for his message.

It is true that you have to allow time for eating, clearing the tables, announcements, and music, but limit your preliminaries so the listeners will not be weary before the speaker begins. Remember, the head can absorb only what the rear end can endure.

At the meeting, when reminding the speaker of the amount of time allowed him, tell him not how long he may speak, but the time to quit. This will be helpful when he glances at his watch.

BE FAIR ABOUT FINANCES

When planning your budget, realize that the speaker has financial obligations. Some missionaries have to support their families by speaking when on furlough. (Too often their supporters stop giving during furlough, expecting them to augment their incomes by speaking.) Other speakers belong to an organization which estimates their value by the amount of money received for speaking. All speakers have the expense of getting to

41

the meeting and taking time from their other responsibilities.

Include an honorarium in your planning. If you are having a potluck, take an offering. If you are having a planned banquet with a set price, charge enough to cover a gift for the speaker.

You realize that I cannot tell you the amount to give because it will vary with the value of money in your area, the size of your group and the prominence of the speaker. And sometimes his attitude toward money.

It is wise to ask a strange speaker if he expects a set amount of money. Some do — perhaps because they have had the unhappy experience of being given less than the expense of getting to the meeting. Yes, it can happen! Especially to out-of-towners. I was asked to another town to speak so that money could be raised for the church's missionary program. Few, if any, outside speakers can afford that expense.

Most speakers will not ask for a set amount but accept whatever is given to them. Personally, I believe the amount given to the speaker is the responsibility of the group who invites him. They know their own finances best. Besides, Scripture says:

"Stay in that one house, sharing their food and drink; for the worker earns his pay. Do not move from house to house. When you come into a town and they make you welcome, eat the food provided for you" (Luke 10:7, 8).

Though this Scripture verse was inspired in an age when money was not widely used, when providing food, drink, and a place to sleep was used instead, the principle is still valid today. It is your responsibility to provide for the speaker, so he may eat and sleep, and it is the responsibility of the speaker to take whatever is given with a thankful heart toward God.

This is the attitude of many, probably most, speakers. They need not demand of people for God balances their budgets, not providing Cadillacs, but paying their bills. One church may be able to give little while another can be generous. Recently in one day I received $10.00 for speaking at a luncheon and $63.41 at an evening meeting. The consecrated speaker learns ". . . my expectation is from him" (Ps. 62:5, KJV).

5

Special Touches

The remembered meal-meeting includes more than food, no matter how delicious, or speaker, no matter how interesting. All meetings provide those two things. You want more than that. Here are some special touches which you can use to make your meeting outstanding.

Here is a suggested program sequence:
  Words of welcome
  Grace
  Meal
  Background music (if time is needed to clear tables)
  Musical selection
  Announcements

Missionary moment
That Something Extra (see following
    suggestions)
Musical selection
Speaker, slides and/or film
Benediction

MUSIC

I believe all the wonderful things said
about music, such as "Music is a discipline,
and a mistress of order and good manners;
she makes the people milder and gentler,
more moral and more reasonable" (Martin
Luther). I even like singing commercials.
They do sell products. I enjoy the stately
hymns, cantatas, and oratorios of the church.
They quiet the heart for worship.

Background music and special numbers
are to a meeting what trimming is to a dress.
Often the buttons or the colorful scarf makes
a woman's outfit attractive, and music pro-
vides the charm that makes the meeting delightful.

Background music sets a pleasing tone to
a meeting. Happy are you if you have a pianist in your group, someone who loves the
Lord sufficiently to provide background music, who will play quietly while people are
assembling, during the offering, and for the

special numbers. Her only gratification may be soul-satisfaction but she is a treasure. Value her.

If no pianist is available, borrow a record player, and assign someone to watch it. Music is a touch that your meeting needs.

Special numbers should be planned with variety in mind. The dear, willing soprano has her place but ask your friends if they know of anything different. Perhaps you will find a mother who sings with her children. A group of this type is especially good for a Mother's Day banquet. Or you may learn of a boy who plays a trumpet. He, too, needs encouragement. What about having the bass from the choir? He might be able to fit the banquet into his schedule and a deep bass singer is always a treat. Besides, there are accordion players, vibraharp players, spoon players, harmonica players. The idea is to have variety by inquiring.

If you have never heard your prospective entertainer sing or play, invite him to play for a Sunday school class first so you will be able to appraise his ability. Mothers who offer their talented children are often prejudiced, highly so.

If your meeting is large, and your budget will allow, give an honorarium to those who provide the music. You will have a better

47

quality of music this way. These people pay for their lessons, the special dress that they wear. You can cry "mercenary" but you cannot change the fact that when a person becomes proficient in his talent, he ceases being an amateur and becomes a professional. Being a professional means he is good enough to receive payment for his work, be it cooking, gardening, or performing.

EXTRAS

Use as many people in the program as possible. You can please everyone if you notice them and use them. Inasmuch as you cannot use everyone in the planning aspects, use as many as possible by letting them have a part in the meeting itself.

The Christian Women's Clubs have an idea which enhances their meetings. They have special displays — someone who shows a button collection, new fashion styles, flower arrangements, or something different. When I speak at one of their meetings I always look forward to the special displays.

Often your extra touch will attract an unexpected guest and that is your goal — the person who doesn't usually attend your meetings.

Hobbies may provide the extra touch. Perhaps some one in your group collects religious stamps (I do), or Bible coins (a friend of mine does), or dolls from many lands (another one of my friends does). Let such collections be shown as part of your program.

Church-oriented items are often available. The missionary society may have an exhibition of things which have been made to give away. The speaker may bring artifacts from the country about which he is speaking. Or one of the Sunday school classes may have made a model of a tabernacle or synagogue which they will be pleased to exhibit.

Commercial groups will provide an exhibit for the advertising value. A florist may be willing to show how to make attractive floral arrangements. A clothing store may show the recent styles. One of the gardening clubs might bring unusual varieties of fuchsias, begonias, or whatever is in season.

Skits may be provided by the dramatic group in your church. Perhaps it has one suitable for a special occasion, such as Mother's Day poems, a biblical theme, or a seasonal subject.

Look around. There is wide variety in this world and as you widen the interests of your group you enlarge the size of it.

GETTING ACQUAINTED

The human tendency is to sit and talk with only those we know, but to do that defeats, in part, the idea behind the group meeting. One of the objectives is to introduce strangers into your group and make friends. So try different ways to mix the crowd.

Have everyone whose last name begins with A, B, or C sit at one table, and so on through the alphabet.

Seat by birthdays with all the January birthdays at one table, and so on.

If you are in a tourist state, such as California, have everyone who came from one certain state, such as Texas, sit at the same table.

If your group consists of young people, line the boys on one side of the room and the girls on the other side, and then have them meet in the middle so that each boy can eat with the girl who happened to be opposite him.

Reach the forgotten people by having a special luncheon for those living in a nearby retirement home. Organize a car committee to pick them up and bring them to the meeting. Don't forget the older men. Give each of the special guests a memento of the occasion, preferably something usable, such as toilet articles, or an edible — dates, soft-centered candy or homemade cookies.

SLIDES 2.

If someone in the church has picture slides of his recent trip, ask him to show twenty (no more) at the meeting. The slides may only be Me in front of the colosseum, Me in front of the catacombs, Me on a misty day, but if too many aren't shown, people are interested in seeing their friends.

You have to use discretion in selecting the person to ask. You know the people in your group who have the reputation of taking forever to say nothing. The most polite way to avoid boredom is to limit the number of slides to be shown.

It may be that your church or group missionary will send you slides from overseas. If so, he should be reimbursed for the slides. Taking slides is an expensive hobby. Whoever shows them should select carefully the slides to use, and project them before he shows them to the group. Slides up-side-down or in disorder do not add to the cause of missions. Hopefully the missionary will suggest an order, but if not, put all the scenic shots together, all the family slides, and all the church slides, or whatever headings seem logical.

Arrange for the projector and screen before the meeting. Who is going to bring what? Set them in place before anyone arrives. Nothing is more distracting to the audience than waiting while the projector is set up and someone fumbles with the focus. Also check whether the extension cord is the right length to extend from the wall plug to the place you want the projector. As insurance, have an extra bulb for the projector on hand. All of these precautions may sound like fussy details but they make the difference between a smoothly run meeting and a hodge-podge which attracts no one to future meetings.

FILMS

You don't always have to have a speaker. If that sounds like heresy, wait a minute. Consider a film. After all, even a variety of speakers can become the same old thing.

There are hundreds of Christian films available on a wide variety of subjects at a wide range of prices. Nearly every denomination and mission board has a film of its work. Individual companies also produce films on general subjects.

For suggestions, look in Christian magazines where these films are advertised, or write the head office of your denomination, or ask your pastor. The interests of your group should lead you to a suitable film.

Order early — someone else may want the film, and there are only a given number available. When the film arrives, have whoever is to show it take the time to preview it. It might contain something unexpected that would prevent your showing it. And also, having seen it, you can advertise the film better.

Afterwards, mail it back promptly. Someone else is waiting for that film.

BOOKS

Meetings are an ideal time to promote Christian books. Most people mean to buy books but they don't take the time to go out of their way to the special book store where Christian books are sold.

Ask a book store owner to bring a selection of books to the meeting and during and at the end of the meeting announce that she is there with a selection of books.

Have a cart displaying your group's library books. All too often people forget to look at the books; therefore, if you have a special book or two that you want your

members to read, appoint someone to go
from table to table with the book selection.

MISSIONS

A little imagination will enable you briefly
to present missions, keeping them in the
minds of the people.

Artifacts. Perhaps your special missionary
can send you different items from the field.
These can be placed on a table, with a small
sign indicating what they are, and someone
can be assigned to stand by the table ex-
plaining the items, or during the meeting
give a brief talk, telling about the items.

Tapes. Send a cassette to your missionary.
Have him speak on it for five, and not more
than ten minutes, and return the cassette to
you. With the volume turned up, play the
cassette during the early part of the meeting.

Missionary letters. Reading a letter is a
regular part of many meetings and usually
is poorly done. The letter is too long, too
wordy, and dull. The person who reads it
snatches it up at the last minute, and mum-
bles the contents in a low voice. This is one
of the best ways to kill interest in missions
and your meeting.

Instead, ask someone to read the letter in advance, and select portions — I repeat, portions — to read at the meeting.

Air forms or birthday cards can be passed around for people to write messages on or sign. As few people know what to write on the spur of the moment, suggest that each one give his favorite Bible verse, or the thing she likes best about the meeting, or why she came to the meeting, or something of interest about the church or Sunday school. Missionaries and their children are always pleased to be remembered.

Bring Christmas presents in October. Christmas is a big time on the mission field and the missionaries always try to do something special. I have never known a missionary who had enough gifts to give one to everyone who attended the local church, or to the children if the missionary runs an orphanage.

The gifts must be mailed early. Consult the missionary about what the local government will allow him to receive. At present I can send practically nothing to Korea but can send to India, up to $5.00 per package. And you have to ask the United States Post Office for the necessary mailing instructions and forms.

The gifts need not be new if they are clean and usable. Enclose them in a plastic bag so they can pass customs, and tie with a flat colored ribbon (bows become flat with the mailing) and a card or tag which tells if the gift is suitable for a boy or a girl, and the suitable age.

Be encouraged. With a little practice, you can develop your skills and become an entrepreneur in the world of meetings, presenting the best for the Lord and His people.

6

Say it Right, Say it Often

This is the day of the population explosion, of the crowd, when it is important to reach as many people as possible with news of your activity. Up to the seating capacity of your meeting place, each additional person requires little extra work. Consider, what is the difference in setting a table for three or for ten?

In order to reach people you have to let them know what is going on, far enough ahead of the selected time so they can plan to attend your special event.

Use every possible means of communication to all prospects. All too often the "in" group knows while the "out" group doesn't, and it is the "out" group who is the most lonesome, the ones who need most to be reached. Always aim to reach the fringe of your group.

PUBLICITY COMMITTEE

Communication is so important and there is so much to do that this should be one of the special committees. The leader should be an ex officio member to guide, prod, and check, but others should do the actual work.

Seek for people with a variety of talents for this committee. You need an extrovert who will do the phoning, a precise person to look after the details, and an artistic person to make the name tags, and such. Nothing takes the place of enthusiasm for getting things going, but for following through the quiet plodder is needed too. The diverse temperaments may become annoyed at each other but this is an opportunity for the members to follow the Scripture verse, "If possible, so far as it lies with you, live at peace with all men" (Rom. 12:18).

MAIL

A short letter or card announcing the event should be prepared. The writer should be certain the information is complete, giving what, where, when (day and time), and who. Include a phone number or card if reservation is required. If the event is to be held at a home give clear and complete directions how to get there. If the directions are complicated (and in many residential districts they are) include a map.

Send to all prospects. Don't try to save postage by omitting someone you think knows about the meeting. I did that when I was sponsor of a teen-age group, and when the leaders found I had not included them in the mailing, they were disgruntled. People like to be remembered. That is why direct mail is such a popular way of selling. It reaches people who can be reached no other way, and at their homes when they have the time to consider what you are presenting. Sell your event by direct mail.

NEWSPAPERS

Presumably the leader requested the speaker, or the company that supplied the film, to send a fact sheet, and perhaps a picture. This is the information the writer will use to prepare a release for the newspapers. In some cases she can use it with very few changes, merely the insertion of date and place.

Prepare and mail the release to all the local newspapers. Check before you mail it to be sure it includes the speaker's topic or the name of the film, and the usual when and where.

As all churches and organizations center their social life around the meal-meeting, the newspaper will receive many similar notices. Therefore look for some unusual feature about the speaker and emphasize it. Often there is an interesting connection between a missionary speaker and the current news of that country. Or it may be that you can tie the speaker into the American news-scene. Any speaker with a topic covering some means of improving human relationships has general interest.

If it is a Mother's Day banquet and you are honoring someone special, mention the person to be honored. Perhaps the oldest mother, the youngest mother, the mother with the youngest child, or the mother of the most prominent member of your church, (the mayor's mother goes to some church) or the mother with the most children who also has time for other people. People are interested in reading about local people.

Special mention is important also with reference to those who will perform the musical numbers. The newspaper editor will be happy if you include their names in your release.

If your speaker is dealing with a current subject, you may be able to arrange for an interview. I am hopeful that whoever is writing the publicity or arranging an interview has become acquainted with the editor of the local paper. Ask for a style sheet and use it. Many rules of grammar are arbitrary and a style sheet gives the editor's preferred mechanical rules for preparing news copy.

You do know you should leave at least one and one-half inch margins on your copy so the editor can make changes, don't you? And also that you put the most important facts first, so the editor can cut your release without omitting any of the important details. The editor is always fighting for space.

If you hope to have special attention paid to your meeting, phone the editor during business hours. Otherwise you are asking him to work overtime without pay. Tell what is different about your speaker. It may be that you can set up a phone call between a reporter and the speaker. Or it may be that the paper will send a reporter to the meeting — and a photographer if it is a community meeting and therefore important. Or the reporter may bring his own camera. Treat him cordially, and give him preference. He is working, and has many stories to cover, while you are getting free advertising. It is probable that the reporter will come, meet the speaker, and be on his way. If you should be fortunate enough, or your function is large enough for him to stay to the meeting, be certain he sits next to the speaker so he can glean extra bits of information while he eats.

Cultivate newspapers. Advertising increases business, it increases attendance at ball games, and it will increase attendance at your church-related events. The newspaper can reach people with your news that you cannot reach any other way.

BULLETIN BOARDS

Practically every church, school, or meeting place has a bulletin board where you can post attractive notices of your event.

You can put a plain typed announcement on the board but it will be overlooked by many people. It is best to have someone make a colorful announcement. It need not be too fancy. You can use cardboard, print neatly, and adorn with pictures cut out from a magazine. If the speaker sent his picture, use it. If the speaker is telling of a certain country the outline of that country may be easy to draw — for instance, Mexico, India,

South America, or Africa. A colorful line drawing will attract attention, and inside the map you can print the details. Or you may find usable pictures in magazines, such as *National Geographic, Life* and sometimes in *Time*.

When the event is over, take the announcement down. Keep the bulletin board from being cluttered. Return the picture to the speaker. It cost him money. Leave room for the next person to make his announcement.

PULPIT ANNOUNCEMENTS

Because your organization is church-related, you will want the pastor to make an announcement from the pulpit. Don't merely expect him to make it. Prepare it. Give him the important facts written down. If possible, hand it to him early Sunday morning, but if you give it to him too far in advance he may misplace it. He is human. And, of course, too late is too late.

CHURCH BULLETIN

In their Sunday bulletin with the order of the service, many churches print announcements. If your church does, the publicity committee should prepare a brief announcement and give it to the church secretary. She is usually responsible for the contents of the bulletin. So that your announcement will be read, start with the fact of the most interest to people — the name of a person, for instance:

Dorothy C. Haskin, former actress and well-known Christian writer, will speak on "How I Found Christ in Hollywood" at the Soul Winners League. The meeting will be held Monday evening, February 28, at 7:45 in the home of Mr. and Mrs. Bert Hawkins, 900028 Hillhurst Drive. Refreshments will be served after the meeting. A cordial invitation is extended to all.

Note: Unless everyone in the church is welcome to attend the meeting, don't announce it in the bulletin.

You should give your announcement to the secretary early in the week so it will be included and also have a prominent place in the bulletin.

Some people wonder why announcements are printed in the bulletin and the minister also makes the announcements. This is because human beings are human beings — variable. Some read the bulletin. Some do not. Some hear the minister. Some sit in the pew with their minds in a dozen other places. If you want your meeting known you have to take every opportunity to advertise it.

RESERVATIONS

If your group meets regularly you know about how many to expect and can plan according. If it is a large occasional group, then you must have reservations to estimate the amount of food needed. However, reservations at best are never completely accurate. Some people who sign up can't come because the unexpected has developed in their lives. And always a few come who didn't make reservations.

If you feel that you need reservations, one member of the publicity committee should be assigned this task. Depending on the size of the budget she may hand-make, mimeograph, or have tickets printed. Reservations may be solicited by direct mail (if a large scattered group), by phone (if a small group), or at other meetings.

When someone is assigned to sell tickets at meetings, too often an announcement is made: "Betty Smith has the tickets," and few people know who Betty Smith is. Even if she is asked to stand, people may get only a dim view of her. It is better for her to wear a small sign saying, "Get your tickets for the What-have-you Banquet from me." Make the price of the banquet an even amount so it will be easy for her to make change. If making change is complicated, she may miss opportunities to sell other tickets.

The reservation member of the publicity committee is also responsible for securing transportation for those who need it. She knows who is coming and therefore it is easier for her to team up people who need a ride with those who have a car and live nearby.

THE NEXT COMING ATTRACTION

The present meeting is one of the best possible places to announce the next meeting. In fact, such an announcement is mandatory. And it is extremely important that the announcement be made properly. If you consider the time and money spent in producing TV commercials you can evaluate properly your group's announcements.

The keynote is brevity and variety.

Cut the announcements to the minimum. People listen to only the first couple of announcements. After that they close their ears as they do when one commercial follows another on the TV screen.

Variety can be achieved by some of the following ways:

Two people. Instead of the leader making all the announcements, variety can be obtained by using two people. The sound of two different voices will hold the attention better than the drone of one voice. Two members can pretend they are talking over the phone, or meeting on the street. One invites the other to the meeting, and answers his questions about the meeting.

Or use a large sign, one yard high and three yards long made on brown wrapping paper. Two people can carry it in, and unfold it.

Skit. Two or more people can present a brief skit announcing the coming event, perhaps a conference. Have a couple come on with too much luggage (that can be funny and a subtle suggestion not to take too much), arriving at camp perhaps at the wrong time, and then being shown around by a guide, who will tell about the interesting points of the coming conference.

Opaque Projector. The standard projector has light behind a slide but an opaque projector reflects light onto a postcard or solid sheet of paper. With this type of projector someone with skill at drawing or lettering can make personal announcements. Perhaps there is a member of your church who has been taught to print clearly, for example, an engineer. With tactful persuasion he will be happy to use his talent for your organization and make attractive signs for you to show on the opaque projector.

These are enough ideas to keep the publicity committee busy for a few months. Remember too that there are many books on the subject of publicity. It is one of America's specialties. Hopefully, this chapter will so interest you that you will go to the public library and get other books on the many phases of public relations.

7

Decorate it Bright

How lovely!

How ego-warming it is when guests entering the meeting place exclaim at its attractiveness. A tastefully decorated room gives its own welcome and reassures the guests that they will enjoy the meeting. It is essential to have the place of meeting as attractive as the leader and committee can make it.

When selecting the decorating committee, the leader has the opportunity to use the talents of many. In a church-related program the more people who cooperate, the more people who have an interest in the event. Here is an opportunity to use people whose talents are definitely different from the abilities of those who worked on the publicity committee. The decoration committee needs people to decorate the tables, make place cards, name tags, and programs.

In a very small church, one person could do all three, but as all of us live busy lives these days, six is a better number, two for each division of the work. Women who cannot sing, are not musical, and not extrovert enough to sell may have usable artistic talent. They will be pleased to use their talents for the Lord, especially as much of this work can be done at home, where, if they have small children, they can be with them and at the same time feel that they are performing a useful service.

TABLE DECORATION

The most simple way to decorate a table is with flowers. Whoever is in charge can phone her friends, church members, and see what is in season that she can use. Use whatever flowers are available, be they geraniums, ferns, ivy, roses. If you live in one of the Western states, cacti make interesting decorations. The practiced hand and eye will find hundreds of ways to use the different flowers.

However, flowers are not available all year round. Fruit is suitable for Thanksgiving, symbolic of the graciousness of God in providing for us. Often in autumn colorful leaves are available.

If the meeting features some foreign country, maps, curios, dolls, artifacts, and objects from the country can be obtained from some member of the group and used for decorations. (See chapter on Foreign Flavored Meetings for additional suggestions.)

NAME TAGS

Name tags are needed for everyone. Few people remember names and it is helpful if a person can, when meeting someone, slyly glance at the name card.

Prepare name tags for the officers, speaker, and committee members before the meeting. These can be handed out when each one arrives. Other tags can be prepared without names. One of the committee members, assigned to stand at the entrance, should write the guest's name on the name tag and pin it on her when each person arrives.

The easy way to do this is to get paper backed with a special adhesive. You write the name of the person on the plain side, peel off the backing and press it on the dress. Most of the time it will stick.

To give these name tags a little color, buy small pictures of flowers which may be glued on each tag.

However, nearly every group has someone artistic enough to make simple symbolic name tags. Buy construction paper and cut out a design that is appropriate to the theme of the meeting or suitable for the time of year. Here are a few simple designs:

One of the most clever name tags I ever received was a pipe cleaner shaped like a clothes-hanger, with my name pinned on it, like this:

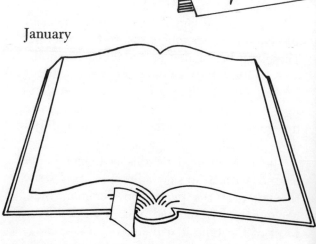

January

February

March

73

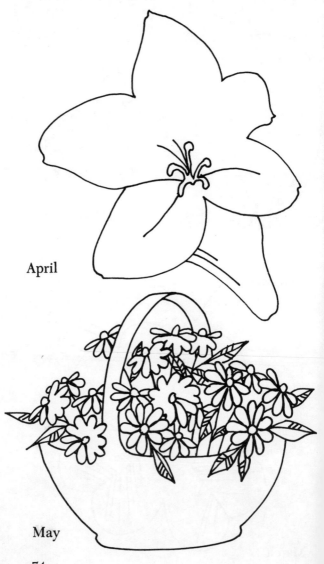

April

May

74

June

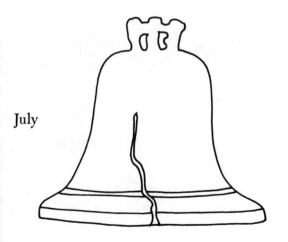

July

75

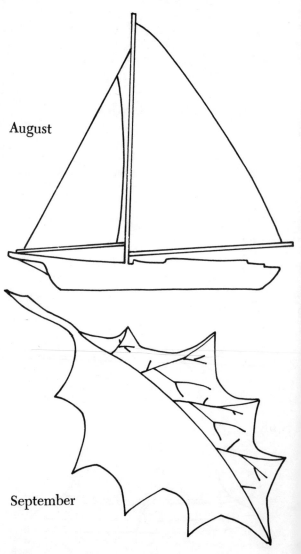

August

September

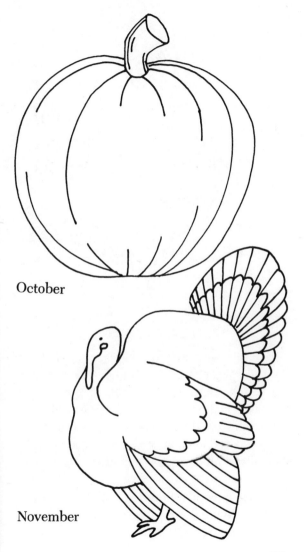

October

November

December

PLACE CARDS

Usually you will need place cards only for the speaker's table — eight or ten according to the length of the table. The easy way to make them is to buy plain cards and write the names on them. You can paste a flower in the corner of each card. Or if your budget will afford it, you can buy decorated place cards.

If you have a little artistic ability you can make individual place cards. Take a white filing card, bend it in the middle so it will

78

stand up. With a felt pen write the person's name boldly on the card. (Check, to be certain you are spelling the person's name correctly. Remember there is Peterson and Petersen, and my name is Haskin, not Haskins, but few people are sufficiently thoughtful to spell it correctly. It is however worth the extra time as people are sensitive about their names.)

In the corner paste a cut-out symbol of the meeting.

Once I attended a banquet where the place cards were long narrow slips of thin cardboard, suitable for later use as bookmarks.

At other times, you may cut out the symbol that you are using for the meeting, and write the name of someone who needs prayer, maybe the ill members of your group, or the missionaries in whom your group is interested. If these are attractive, they will be carried home, and serve as prayer reminders.

An encouraging place card is one with a Bible verse. You might write it on a plain piece of paper, roll it like a scroll, and hold in place with a tiny piece of scotch tape. Or type it on a book-shaped piece of paper.

Those of us who attend church-related meetings enjoy the comfort of Bible verses.

If possible, select short verses that you can print or type out. If you use references, everyone will not look up the references because all people are not equally acquainted with the Bible. Use a number of verses so persons seated near each other will all have different verses. Always use comforting verses. (No one wants to be warned of bad times or impending doom at a banquet.) Here are a few suggestions (using the King James Version):

"Unto thee, O LORD, do I lift up my soul" (Ps. 25:1).

"Wait on the LORD: be of good courage, and he shall strengthen thine heart: wait, I say, on the LORD" (Ps. 27:14).

"Rejoice in the LORD, O ye righteous: for praise is comely for the upright" (Ps. 33:1).

"Be glad in the LORD, and rejoice, ye righteous: and shout for joy, all ye that are upright in heart" (Ps. 32:11).

"I will bless the LORD at all times: his praise shall continually be in my mouth" (Ps. 34:1).

"O magnify the LORD with me, and let us exalt his name together" (Ps. 34:3).

"I sought the LORD, and he heard me, and delivered me from all my fears" (Ps. 34:4).

"They looked unto him, and were lightened: and their faces were not ashamed" (Ps. 34:5).

"God is our refuge and strength, a very present help in trouble" (Ps. 46:1).

"Cast thy burden upon the LORD, and he shall sustain thee: he shall never suffer the righteous to be moved" (Ps. 55:22).

"Make a joyful noise unto God, all ye lands" (Ps. 66:1).

"Thou shalt guide me with thy counsel, and afterward receive me to glory" (Ps. 73:24).

"For the LORD God is a sun and shield: the LORD will give grace and glory: no good thing will he withhold from them that walk uprightly" (Ps. 84:11).

The Book of Psalms is filled with wonderful verses. These are but a few of the appropriate ones. Revel through the Psalms and you will find many delightful verses.

PROGRAMS

A printed or mimeographed program is a special help to the person in charge. It limits the number of announcements. With such a program the leader should have to announce only the first number, and then the meeting should follow according to the program. (The leader should warn the participants that there will be no separate announcements.) This cuts out dead spots in a meeting.

The cover of the program should be of construction paper. If it is 8½-by-5½-inches, you can get two covers out of each sheet of construction paper. On the cover should be pasted the motif that is being used in the other decorations.

Inside there should be the menu, the order of the meeting, words of any hymn to be sung, and special announcements. As an extra touch, if you serve special food, the recipe may be included. Women are always pleased to get a new recipe and this will prompt them to keep the program as a memento.

Does it sound like work? Well, many hands make light work and if the decoration committee gets together to make the table decorations, name tags, place cards, and program, the members will enjoy being together, and much work will be easily accomplished.

8

The Big Moment

The meeting is your big moment — are you ready for it?

In order to be a leader in public you need a certain amount of training. But you haven't had it! Up to now you have been a housewife, mother, and Sunday school teacher and no one has paid too much attention to you.

But here is your opportunity to do something noteworthy for the Lord. The meeting which you have planned will serve to strengthen other Christians and interest the uncommitted to Christ. Therefore, you must be ready to be your best in public. Nothing takes the place of experience but there are certain things which you can do at home which will help you to have confidence in public.

APPEARANCE

What you wear is important.

Don't wear a dress so bright that it will distract from what you are saying. People should be conscious of what you represent, not your clothes.

Don't wear a dress so old-fashioned that strangers will think Christians are dowdy. When I first became a Christian I immediately began wearing long-sleeved dresses because I thought all Christians were supposed to look that way. It was a couple of years later that I learned, ". . . a peculiar people, zealous of good works" (Titus 2:14, KJV), a quotation which some people use to justify odd clothes. However, it is not what we wear, but our attitude of helpfulness that distinguishes us from the average selfish person.

Don't wear a dress that is immodest, that is too short, with skirt slit too high, or neckline cut too low, so that people will think, "She doesn't dress like a Christian." We are admonished that "Women . . . must dress in a becoming manner, modestly . . ." (I Tim. 2:9).

Don't wear a sleeveless dress if you are over forty. If you do, when you raise your arms the loose, repulsive fat will bounce back and forth.

Don't wear dangling earrings, which will catch people's attention and they will concentrate on them, instead of on what you are saying.

Do wear a familiar dress, one that you have worn so often that you will not feel ill at ease in it.

Do be alert to every detail of your dress, that your scarf (if you wear one) is pinned properly in place, that the zipper is closed (sometimes we can't quite reach and plan to have someone do it for us later), that the dress is freshly pressed. All these details are important.

Do plan to take time to dress so that your hair will be combed neatly, your nails freshly manicured and, if you wear make-up, that it is applied so it looks natural.

Do stand in front of a full-length mirror before you leave the house. See if your slip is showing or if you have on too many ornaments. See if you give one pleasing effect with your clothes.

Do remember you can't please everyone. No matter how careful you are and what you wear, someone won't like it. But that is a fact of life. So do your best and remind yourself that we all have differences of opinion.

VOICE

". . . if the trumpet-call is not clear, who will prepare for battle?" (I Cor. 14:8) is a reminder of the importance of speaking clearly. If your utterances yield no clear meaning, how can anyone know what to do? You will be talking to yourself. Nothing in the world is altogether soundless but unless I understand the sound, it is gibberish to me.

Few people speak clearly. They mumble, or look around or down when they speak. Often, during a conversation you know what a person says because you have an idea of what he is going to say, not because you actually hear his words. But a leader must be understood clearly. You are eager for the gifts of the Spirit, so aspire to excel in those which build up the church (I Cor. 14:9-12).

Speaking clearly is a talent which you can cultivate. Actors and actresses spend endless hours repeating phrases to give them the correct expression, or to rid themselves of an undesirable regional accent. If a tape recorder is available to you, make a tape and listen to it until you cease to be self-conscious about the sound of your voice, and can correct your grammatical errors and slurring pronunciation. Do you talk too fast? If you do, slow up. Learn not only to pronounce words but also to enunciate.

For clarity practice phrases like the old-tongue-twisters, "Peter Piper picked a peck of pickles," "Black bugs blood," or "Around the rocks the ragged rascals ran."

When you have become accustomed to the sound of your own voice, then practice your announcements in front of a mirror. Repeat them over and over again until you can say them clearly and distinctly. Practice especially the strange and foreign words so you won't trip on them in public.

Also watch your hands. Keep them down to your side, or resting easily on the lectern. Fluttering hands or absentmindedly scratching yourself will detract from what you have to say.

This is a form of self-improvement that will make you better liked not only in meetings, but also in every phase of your social life.

BREVITY

This is the day of enforced brevity — life is too full. Even so, brevity always has been appreciated. Cicero, a Roman statesman who lived before the time of Jesus Christ, wrote,

\\ "Brevity is the great charm of eloquence."

Shakespeare said, "Brevity is the soul of wit" using the word wit not in the sense of joke but referring to the ability to reason.

You, yourself, must first be convinced that a clear, concise statement will be listened to more often than a rambling announcement. Write out what you have to say, and partially memorize it so with a mere glance at the paper you can make the announcement, clearly and completely.

Also, when asking people to perform, insist on brevity. Suggest that the singer sing two verses, or ask for a *short* poem. The program will be packed so it must move smoothly and quickly. Each person should take only his fair share of the time. If one person takes too much time the rest of the meeting will be behind schedule.

It takes tact to convince others that they should be brief. But if you genuinely like people, both those who take part and those in the audience, you will be fair to both, and in a friendly manner suggest brevity to all participants.

You set the example. When you have finished making a statement, stop.

"I love a finished speaker,
O yes, indeed I do.

I don't mean one who's polished,
I just mean one who's through."

PRAYER

According to the size of your group you can either say grace, the opening prayer, and the benediction yourself, or ask three different people to participate.

Be thoughtful when you ask someone to pray in public. Ask her privately and ask in such a manner that she can feel free to refuse if she wishes. Many people are embarrassed to pray in public because they do not do it often enough. Never press anyone to pray publicly. Prayer is to God and must be a matter between the individual and the Lord.

When you do ask someone, suggest she write out her prayer. This will help her to be less embarrassed and to be brief.

Grace is giving thanks for food, not a prayer for the entire meeting. Here are a few suggested ways of saying grace:

"Dear Lord, come be our guest,
Then we know our food is blessed. Amen."

"Bless, O Father, thy gifts to our use and us to thy service. Give us grateful hearts for all thy mercies and make us mindful of the needs of others, through Jesus Christ, our Lord, Amen."

"Bless us, O Lord, and these thy gifts, which, of thy bounty we are about to receive. In Jesus name. Amen."

"For these, and all His mercies, God's holy Name be praised. Through Christ our Lord. Amen."

Prayer for the meeting should come after the meal is eaten. It may be either formal, extemporaneous, or a combination of both.

There are things to be said in favor of both types of prayer. Presumably extemporaneous prayer comes from the heart and expresses what the person actually feels. Actually it may be stiff and self-conscious. It takes experience to close the mind to all outside influences and to concentrate only on God. Often women who work with church or church-related organizations have few opportunities to pray in public. Therefore a prayer worded ahead of time makes for ease.

Formal prayers, found in books, often express thoughts that one would not think of when nervous. Even in my own devotions I often use formal prayers which express a greater consecration than I had thought of, and to them add my own petitions.

In the general prayer, the person should pray for the singers, special touches, speaker, and that God may bring each one present closer to Him.

Benediction, too, should be brief, thanking the Lord for the blessing of the meeting, and asking His continued blessing on all as they go home and return to their various tasks.

LISTS, LISTS, LISTS

The day before the meeting go over the lists in your notebook and see that you have attended to everything. Then make two lists for the meeting day.

To Do list. List people you should phone as a last minute reminder. Note that you must check the microphone and the projector before the meeting. These things will accumulate and vary with the meeting. As an example, I am giving a luncheon next week; I have to check

    Extra tables

    Large serving spoons

    Sufficient plastic eating utensils

    Change for the girl taking the money

    Letters to read during the meeting

    Extension cord to hook up the electric cooker (where the chili another woman and I have made will be heated).

I don't have to worry about the decorations. The woman who does that for me at each meeting is perfectly dependable. Nor do I have to be concerned about those who are bringing the salads and crackers. I have worked with them long enough to trust them. The list covers the things which I must attend to myself.

To Say list. Have a complete outline of the program, and notes as to what you will say about singer, speaker, or special touches. Don't burden yourself with extra thinking at the meeting. (And don't wait until the last minute to ask the speaker what you should say about him. It is only courtesy to have long since made the necessary inquiries.)

TIME

Begin on time. Everyone will never arrive on time but if you wait for everyone to get there, you can be as much as an hour late in starting. Ten minutes leeway is the most you should ever allow. As your group becomes aware of the fact that the meeting will begin on time, they will be more apt to be on time. And why should the prompt person be penalized by waiting for the late person?

Stop on time. It is true that American women do not have to rush home to get dinner. Hubbies are trained to wait or to accept TV dinners. However, some women have children who must be picked up after school or after a lesson, and if these women are delayed they will not feel free to come again. If you stop at the appointed time, those who must leave will leave and those who don't have to will stand around, enjoying talking with each other.

ENJOY YOURSELF

Have I frightened you by telling you the hundred right things to do? Don't let me. These are only suggestions. If you take them, they will help your meeting to run more smoothly, but after all, you are among friends and they will excuse many a slip.

If you have done all you can, then sit down and watch your successful meal-meeting unfold, each thought-out step by each thought-out step. There is enough food, the music was delightful, the speaker was prompt and interesting and everyone enjoyed himself or herself.

AFTER THE MEETING

Show appreciation. Thank all your committee members. Thank the Lord that you were able to serve your fellow Christians, the stranger who attended, and the Lord Himself. And thank yourself by promising that you will never do it again.

Start on the next meal-meeting program. The next morning, when you are alone with the Lord, and you realize that you have, with His help, done something worthwhile, promise Him that the next time you are asked to organize a meal-meeting program, you will agree to do it, with confidence in Him and knowledge born of experience.

9

Banquet Programs

Throughout this book meal-meetings have been discussed in general, with suggestions suitable for a banquet of any season. Your group may follow these suggestions at a monthly meeting or at a yearly special occasion. A typical program is suggested in the chapter on "Special Touches." But there will be times when you want something different, something to stir mission concern. The following are suggestions for four foreign-flavored meetings.

CHINA CALLS

1. Have a missionary from Hong Kong or Taiwan (Formosa) as speaker.

2. Ask him to bring artifacts such as bowls, vases or clothes. Or inquire if anyone in your group has articles from these places. In these days of travel you may find someone who has brought home interesting souvenirs.

3. If the missionary is a woman, ask her to wear a *cheongsam* (a Chinese woman's dress).

 4. Decorate the invitations with an easy-to-draw Chinese character (written word) like the one sketched. This is the character for people. It is the sign for mouth — perhaps used to designate people because each person is another mouth.

5. Add a colorful touch to the announcement in the church bulletin by using the same character. If it is either mimeographed or printed by offset, make a drawing of the character and use it. If, however, the bulletin is printed by letter press, and you cannot use the character, perhaps the printer has a font of type with an Oriental look. He can print the announcement with this type.

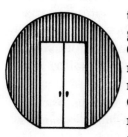

6. Change the door through which the congregation comes into a Chinese door. The Chinese are noted for their moon or round doors. Out of heavy cardboard make a circle large enough to encircle the entrance door and paint it Chinese red.

7. Hang Chinese lanterns around the room for atmosphere. (Remember Japanese and Chinese lanterns are not alike. Japanese lanterns are oval. Chinese lanterns are square or oblong with tassels hanging from them.)

8. Pass out prayer requests in the shape of butterflies. Cut the butterflies from yellow construction paper. Using India ink, print a prayer request on each one. Have enough for each

99

person who attends to take one home with him.

9. Decorate the table with carnations made of Kleenex, and artificial leaves and butterflies made of thin rice paper. Perch the butterflies on top of the carnations.

Directions for making carnations:

(1) Buy a box of colored facial tissues such as Kleenex, pipe cleaners (one for each carnation), green crepe paper.

(2) Cut one tissue in half.

(3) Separate the layers.

(4) Place layers on top of each other.

(5) Accordion pleat, that is, fold lower side, then upper side, until completely pleated.

(6) Wind a long pipe cleaner around the center. This becomes the stem.

(7) With pinking scissors or with ordinary scissors make cuts along edges, one-fourth inch deep, making a fringe.

(8) Pull all layers upward, forming flower.

(9) Wrap green crepe paper around whatever pipe cleaner shows as stem.

10. For refreshments serve tea and fortune cookies, which you can buy from a Chinese grocery store or restaurant. Or if the

meeting includes dinner, serve Chinese food ordered from the local Chinese restaurant.

11. Fold the paper napkins like fans.
Directions:
(1) Buy paper napkins size 13" x 13" coffee stirrers 4½ x 3/8 x 1/12" (one for each fan).
(2) Fold in half.
(3) Accordion pleat.
(4) Insert stirrer among folds at one end of napkin.
(5) Staple together.
(6) Spread out like fan.

This is large enough for the person to use as a napkin and also makes a simple favor to take home.

12. You will get ideas of your own and the flavor needed for the meeting, if you study the pictures in a book or even a travel folder on Hong Kong or Taiwan.

AN EVENING IN FRANCE

1. Invite as speaker a missionary to France. Or have someone prepare a message on France by reading *Let Europe Hear* by Robert Evans, Moody Press ($5.95). Or have a missionary in France send you a tape recording for the meeting.

2. Cut out silhouettes of the Eiffel Tower and paste on invitations (see sketch).

3. Add a sketch of Eiffel Tower to the announcement in the church bulletin.

4. Prior to the speaker, have a fashion show of haute couture.

5. For refreshments serve coffee and le croissants (or the nearest you can find to these delicious French crescents) or French bread and cheese.

6. Get men to serve as waiters. They should wear long white aprons and black ties.

7. Serve the refreshments in a cafe atmosphere. Use small tables, (folding tables will do) with two chairs to each table.

8. Write to U.S. Chamber of Commerce, 21 Avenue George, Paris, France, for posters. (It will take about two months to get these so plan ahead.) Or ask a travel agency for posters. Decorate the meeting place with these posters.

9. Cut out pictures of France from travel

magazines and put on the wall, arranging them to look as if hung in a museum. This can be your petit Louvre.

10. Have someone with artistic talent draw a shop window on a large sheet of white paper. The window should appear flat and small. A few objects, as if placed with air, can be drawn in it. The word *Parfums* in script should be on the glass.

11. Have someone print the following facts on large white cards and pin them up on the walls.

"In many parts of France there is as much need to preach Christianity as there is in any missionary territory" (*Life World Library FRANCE*, p. 117).

"Though Europe contains 15 percent of the world's population only 2 percent of North America's missionaries serve there" (*Let Europe Hear* by Robert Evans, p. 17).

"Europe receives the smallest share of the world missionary dollar" (Ibid., p. 30).

"Approximately 65 percent of the men in France are agnostics" (*World Missions*, Dr. Clyde Taylor, p. 19).

JOURNEY TO JAPAN

1. Have a missionary from Japan as speaker.

2. Ask him to bring Japanese curios.

3. If a woman, ask her to wear *kimono* and *obi*.

4. Ask if the missionary children can sing in Japanese.

5. Issue invitations on fan-shaped pieces of colored paper.

6. Include with the announcement in the bulletin a sketch of fans.

7. Make a *torii* out of heavy cardboard, paint it black and set outside the door of the room in which the meeting is held. The *torii* is the sign of a Shinto shrine.

8. Hang Japanese lanterns profusely around the room. (These are obtainable in any large city in the United States and through some mail order houses.)

9. Serve the refreshments on a low table. (Most churches have one in the nursery department.)

10. Decorate the table with a typical flower arrangement. (Get a book from the public library on Japanese flower arrangements.)

11. Have the hostesses wear *kimono* if possible.

12. Seat hostesses on cushions at each end of the table.

13. Serve tea, almonds, fried shrimp and rice. (There may be a Japanese grocery store in your town where you can buy other authentic foods.)

14. Use chopsticks or *hashi*. (Have a few forks handy for those who are not courageous enough to try using *hashi*.)

GUATEMALA GATHERING

1. Invite as speaker either a missionary from Guatemala on furlough or a Guatemalan studying in the United States.

2. Suggest that the speaker bring whatever artifacts he may have of Guatemala, such as flags, woven cloth or pottery.

3. Issue invitations shaped like the map of Guatemala (see sketch).

4. Add sketch to the announcement in the church bulletin.

5. Ask the speaker, if a woman, to wear the national dress of the tribe with which she works. There are more than twenty Indian tribes in Guatemala and each one has its own distinctive dress.

6. Arrange to have a marimba player for the music. (The marimba is the national instrument of Guatemala.)

7. Teach the group to sing a simple song in Spanish (the national language of Guatemala). For instance:

> *Yo tengo a Christo, Christo en mi corazon*
> *En mi corazon*
> *En mi corazon*
> *Yo tengo a Christo, Christo en mi corazon*
> *Pues yo se que me salvo.*

These words are sung to the tune of "I have joy, joy in my heart" and translate:

> I have Christ, Christ in my heart
> In my heart
> In my heart
> I have Christ, Christ in my heart
> Because I know He saved me.

8. Use bananas as table decorations. If you are using place cards, make them out of yellow construction paper and shape them like bananas.

9. Make an idol out of heavy wrapping paper and place it in a prominent place. (You can find a picture of a Guatemalan idol in *The World Book Encyclopedia* or another encyclopedia.)

10. Decorate the room with bougainvillea if in season.

11. Serve coffee, tamales, beans, corn, sweet potatoes and bananas for refreshments.

12. Have the facts under the heading "Glimpses of Guatemala" printed on a large white card and tacked on the wall.

Glimpses of Guatemala

Guatemala is about the size of Louisiana.

The population is about three and one-half million, the same as Chicago.

Sixty percent of the people are Indian and 40 percent are *Ladinos,* or those with white, Negro and/or Indian blood.

Spanish is the official language. In addition there are twenty languages spoken by different Indian tribes. Missionaries are working on translations in all of these languages. Twelve are being reduced to writing, and the New Testament has been translated into four languages.

There have been sixty revolutions in Guatemala in the last twenty years.

The illiteracy rate throughout Guatemala is 62.3 percent while among the *evangelicos* (those belonging to Protestant churches) it is 25 percent.

The per capita income is $163 per year.

There are twenty-five missionary agencies working in Guatemala.

There were one thousand *evangelico* congregations in 1961 with a total church membership of about eighty thousand or 2 percent of the population. During Evangelism-in-Depth, a nationwide evangelistic campaign in 1962, a conservative estimate of fifteen thousand joined churches.

There are twelve Bible schools or seminaries, and between thirty-five and forty parochial schools, mostly on the primary level.

The national church-going Protestants are active. Most, if not all, the missions are following through on indigenous programs. For instance, while the Friends have twelve missionaries in Guatemala, the sixty-three organized churches are a national organization; the Church of the Nazarene is fully organized under national leadership; several indigenous Pentecostal assemblies were in existence before the first Assemblies of God missionary arrived in 1937. TESCA is a national organization to promote national *evangelico* schools. There is religious freedom in Guatemala.

These are a few suggestions for variety in luncheons and banquets. Once you have supervised a few meals and can be calm in your spirit, the Lord will bring other ideas to your mind.

I don't wish you "luck," (that's what the non-Christian wants). Instead, I commend you and your Christian service to the Lord, reminding you to "Commit to the LORD all that you do and your plans will be fulfilled" (Prov. 16:3).

Lets plan a program 45

Prayer page   TY